6/30/09
$23.93
B·T
JNF

Amazing Animal Defenses

Animal Mimics

Look-Alikes and Copycats

Susan K. Mitchell

Enslow Publishers, Inc.
40 Industrial Road
Box 398
Berkeley Heights, NJ 07922
USA

http://www.enslow.com

These books are dedicated to Emily, who inspired the author.

Library of Congress Cataloging-in-Publication Data
Mitchell, Susan K.
  Animal mimics : look-alikes and copycats / By Susan K. Mitchell.
     p. cm. — (Amazing animal defenses)
  Includes bibliographical references and index.
  Summary: "Find out how animals mimic other, and more dangerous animals to keep themselves safe from predators"—Provided by publisher.
  ISBN 978-0-7660-3293-4
  1. Protective coloration (Biology)—Juvenile literature. 2. Mimicry (Biology)—Juvenile literature. I. Title.
  QL767.M58 2009
  591.47'3—dc22

                                      2008011449

ISBN-10: 0-7660-3293-0

Printed in the United States of America

10 9 8 7 6 5 4 3 2 1

To Our Readers:
We have done our best to make sure all Internet Addresses in this book were active and appropriate when we went to press. However, the author and the publisher have no control over and assume no liability for the material available on those Internet sites or on other Web sites they may link to. Any comments or suggestions can be sent by e-mail to comments@enslow.com or to the address on the back cover.

♻ Enslow Publishers, Inc., is committed to printing our books on recycled paper. The paper in every book contains 10% to 30% post-consumer waste (PCW). The cover board on the outside of each book contains 100% PCW. Our goal is to do our part to help young people and the environment, too!

Cover photo-illustration: Gino Santa Maria/Fotolia, Alia Luria/iStockphoto
Interior photos: Alamy/mikeos, p. 4; Alamy/Bruce Coleman, Inc., pp. 11, 26 (right); Alamy/John Cancalosi, p. 12 (left); Alamy/Peter Arnold, Inc., pp. 12 (right), 14; Alamy/ Steven Haggard, p. 15; Alamy/David Chapman, p. 17; Alamy/Scott Camazine, p. 21 (left); Alamy/imagebroker, p. 22; Alamy/Danita Delimont, p. 26 (left); Alamy/Martin Shields, p. 29; Alamy/John T. Fowler, p. 31; Alamy/Brandon Cole Marine Photography, pp. 34, 38 (left), 41 (left and right); Alamy/WaterFrame, p. 36; Alamy/Chris Rout, p. 38 (right); Alamy/Stan Kujawa, p. 43; Animals Animals–Earth Scenes/Patti Murray, p. 21 (right); Birdforum/Mehd Halaouate, p. 37; Devin Edmonds, p. 32 (left and right); iStockphoto/Alia Luria, p. 1; iStockphoto/Nicola Vernizzi, p. 8; iStockphoto/Alan Lemire, p. 18; iStockphoto/Audrey Roorda, p. 19; iStockphoto/Sven Klaschik, p. 25; Minden Pictures/Michael & Patricia Fogden, p. 20; L. Newman & A. Flowers, p. 6; U.S. Air Force, p. 44.

Contents

Chapter 1   See You Later, Imitator!

In the animal world, being a copycat can be a good thing. Some animals have colors or body shapes that help them hide. This camouflage keeps them safe from predators that want to eat them. For some other animals, their color and shape do not help them hide at all. But they are protected in another way—they mimic other animals.

4

Looking like a snake helps keep the hawk moth caterpillar safe. Most hungry predators would probably avoid this scary-looking creature.

To mimic means to look or act like something else. Many animals "copy" the way other animals look. This confuses and warns predators. Some mimics look like dangerous animals. Others look like things that taste bad or are poisonous. Either way, it can help keep them from becoming lunch.

It can be hard to tell camouflage and mimicry apart. For example, some animals have bodies that look like leaves or sticks. This is camouflage, not mimicry. These animals do look like something else, but they are using their shape and color to hide. True mimics do not hide at all. They can usually be seen very easily.

Mimics have a few ways of fooling predators. Sometimes they are brightly colored to mimic poisonous animals. These colors warn other animals to stay away. There are other mimics that have the shape of more dangerous

Most fish will avoid a poisonous sea slug (left). They also avoid its mimic, a harmless flatworm (right). Having the same appearance helps keep the flatworm safe.

animals, such as snakes, ants, or wasps. For a predator, it can be hard to tell the difference between a mimic and a truly dangerous animal. So they usually leave both the dangerous animals and their look-alikes alone.

In Plain Sight

There are two main kinds of mimics. They are called Batesian and Mullerian. Each kind is named after the scientist who discovered it. Henry Bates was a British scientist. In the 1800s, he took a trip to the Amazon jungle in South America. While he was there, Bates gathered many kinds of butterflies. He had a problem putting them in groups, however. He noticed that there were many kinds of butterflies that looked very similar. Bates had to study them closely.

He learned that some of the butterflies were bad-tasting. Birds and animals knew not to eat them. There were also butterfly mimics that looked like the bad-tasting ones. They, too, were left alone by other animals. In this kind of mimicry, an animal that is usually safe to eat looks like one that is not safe.

Years later, a scientist named Dr. Fritz Muller discovered that Bates was only partly right. Dr. Muller found that mimics were not always harmless. Sometimes even the mimic

This Is a Warning!

Super-bright colors are useful for many things in the animal world. They can help an animal attract a mate. Mostly, however, bright colors mean DANGER! Some animals with colorful bodies are poisonous. Others are bad-tasting or stinky. Either way, they are not a welcome treat to eat. They have no need to hide.

There are many animals that use warning colors. Many snakes, insects, frogs, and ocean animals are brightly colored. The warning colors are usually red, orange, or yellow. One taste of the brightly colored animals and predators quickly learn to stay away from them.

was dangerous. In this type of mimicry, two dangerous animals looked the same. By looking the same, neither is eaten more often than the other.

Mimicry needs a few things to work well. First, both the mimic and the animal it copies have to live in the same area.

Next, it helps if the mimic animal also acts like the animal it is copying. It is not enough to just look like it. For example, there are many kinds of spiders that mimic ants. By lifting two of

Wild FACT Most predators leave ants alone. Some baby insects look like ants, including katydid babies (called nymphs). This helps keep them safe.

their eight legs, they look like six-legged ants. Most ants taste bad or can give a nasty sting, so many animals do not eat them. By acting and looking like an ant, the spider may escape being eaten also.

What Big EYES You Have!

Some animals use a defense called self-mimicry. In self-mimicry, one part of the animal's body looks like another. For example, many types of caterpillar have tail-ends that look exactly like their heads. This gives them a greater chance of surviving an attack. Predators almost always attack the head of their prey, which is a good way to kill it. If the predator accidentally attacks the tail end of a self-mimicking caterpillar, that caterpillars has a chance to get away.

Wild FACT One type of South American toad has two big, dark spots on its rear end that look like eyes! When it is scared, it puts its head down and its rear up in the air.

Other mimics use fake "eyes" called eye spots. An owl butterfly is a very good example. It has one large dark spot on each bottom wing. With the wings fully opened, it looks like the face

The eye spots on an owl butterfly's wings make it look like an owl—an animal most predators would avoid.

of an owl. This can confuse a predator looking for a snack.

Eye spots can also help an animal live through an attack since predators usually try to grab an animal by the head. If the eye spots are far enough from the animal's head, the predator may be fooled into attacking the eye spot area instead. This means the mimic might have a chance to get away with nothing more than a nibble on its tail or wing.

11

Chapter 2

Looks Like Trouble

Red on yellow kills a fellow. Red on black is a friend of Jack. There are several catchy rhymes to help tell a dangerous coral snake from a harmless king snake. They all describe the color patterns of the coral snake, as well as the harmless snake that mimics it. Both of these snakes have red, black, and yellow bands on their bodies.

The very deadly coral snake has red bands next to yellow bands. Certain kinds of king snakes mimic those colors. They have red bands

At first glance, it can be hard to tell a dangerous coral snake (left) from a harmless king snake (right).

next to black bands. Either way, no predator would want to get close enough to find out if it really is a coral snake. This is an example of Batesian mimicry, which is a harmless animal mimicking a dangerous one. By having the color of the coral snake, the mimic stays nice and safe.

Some king snakes also mimic the body shape of a coral snake. Most snakes have heads that are wider than their bodies, but coral snakes have very slim heads that are the exact same size as their bodies. The Mexican milk snake is one type of king snake that mimics the body shape of a coral snake.

Got Milk Snake?

With its red, yellow, and black bands and its body shape, the Mexican milk snake is one of

Wild FACT King snakes are very popular pets. Snake owners like their beautiful colors. They are also very easy to care for.

Big Bluffs

Some snakes mimic only the behavior of dangerous snakes, not their body colors. They often pretend to be deadly when they are really harmless. For example, the harmless bull snake often makes a hissing noise if bothered. It can also vibrate its tail. Together,

the hiss and tail are much like the sounds of a deadly rattlesnake.

The bull snake will also coil up like a rattlesnake to try and scare predators away. All in all, it does a pretty good impression of a rattlesnake. But if that does not work, the bull snake will actually strike at a predator! Bull snakes are constrictors, which means they squeeze their food to death. In other words, they have no venom and are not dangerous. Still, a bite from a bull snake could be very painful.

the best coral snake mimics. This clever mimic is found mostly in the southern parts of Texas and parts of Mexico. Mexican milk snakes share that area with the Texas coral snake.

Both snakes are really shy. Even though the Texas coral snake moves around during the day, it stays hidden. The Mexican milk snake hides also. Both snakes usually stay under piles of leaves. Sometimes they hide among logs or tree stumps. But with their bright warning colors, they would be safe even without hiding. Most predators know to stay away even if the snakes are out in the open.

The Mexican milk snake mimics both the colors and the body shape of a coral snake.

Quite a Mouthful

In a weird twist, there are some king snakes that actually eat coral snakes! Otherwise, the coral snake has very few enemies. Hawks and other large birds are the biggest threats. Animals have learned over time to stay away from the dangerous bright-colored coral snakes and their mimics.

Wild FACT The eastern milk snake is another kind of king snake. But this one does not look like a coral snake. It has colors and patterns that help it mimic another dangerous snake, the copperhead.

But the same colors that protect king snakes can also harm them. Since they look so much like coral snakes, people often kill them. People see the bright colors and panic. They kill the snake before checking to see if it might be a mimic or not.

Tiny But Fierce

Snakes are not the only animals that can mimic other snakes. Some of the best snake mimics are much tinier than any snake. They are caterpillars. Many caterpillars will raise the front of their bodies up in the air when threatened. To many other animals, this looks like a snake.

One of the most amazing of these mimics is the hawk moth caterpillar. This caterpillar can puff up its tail end. This makes the tail end look like the head of a snake.

The hawk moth caterpillar also has a big black spot on each side of its tail end. These eye spots look like scary snake eyes. If that is not enough to frighten off predators, the caterpillar will move its body back and forth like a snake.

Chapter 3 A Bitter Bug to Swallow

Butterflies are some of the most beautiful insects in the world. Very few of them are dangerous to humans. However, there are some butterflies that no animal would dare eat. These butterflies taste very bitter and bad. One of those butterflies is the monarch. Its bright orange and black markings warn birds

Both the monarch butterfly (left) and the viceroy butterfly (below) are bad-tasting and harmful to birds. The best way to tell them apart is to look for the black line going across the wing of the viceroy.

and other animals to stay away. Eating a monarch can make a bird very sick.

The viceroy butterfly has the same colors as the monarch. This helps protect it from birds that have learned that monarchs are bad to eat. For many years, scientists thought the viceroy was not harmful to birds. Now, they have learned that the viceroy is bad tasting, and can also make birds sick. Both butterflies are harmful to birds, and both are protected by looking alike. This is an example of Mullerian mimicry.

Wild FACT

The viceroy is more than a mimic—it is the state butterfly of Kentucky!

Disgusting Disguises

Not surprisingly, very few animals want to eat poop. This is a good thing for some caterpillars and spiders. There are many caterpillars that mimic bird droppings! Their bodies are dark with white patches, and they often have lumpy, bumpy body coverings. It is no wonder that birds do not pay any attention to these caterpillars. It sounds gross, but looking like poop is very good mimicry!

Some types of spiders have the same black-and-white coloring. These spiders will also often tuck their legs close to their bodies. This helps them look even more like a blob of bird droppings. The crab spider (left) is one of them.

You Are What You Eat

Monarch and viceroy butterflies may look the same, but when they are caterpillars they definitely do not. The monarch caterpillar has bands that are black, yellow, and white. The viceroy caterpillar is brown with white splotches on its body. This makes it look very much like bird droppings. Believe it or not, this is a form of mimicry, too. The viceroy caterpillar mimics the look of something yucky that no animal would want to eat.

The food they eat as caterpillars is what makes the monarch and viceroy poisonous. The milkweed plant is the only food a monarch caterpillar eats. It is full of toxins.

Monarch (left) and viceroy (right) caterpillars look very different. But as butterflies, they look very similar.

This Might Sting a Little

Butterflies are not the only bugs that mimic. Many types of flying insects mimic bees or wasps. Few animals eat bees or wasps because of their painful sting. Insects that copy the colors and body shape of a wasp or bee, such as the longhorn beetle (below), are safe also.

Wasps usually have brightly colored bodies. Some are bright red or orange. Others have black and yellow stripes. Some flies and moths have these same colors, as well as a wasp-shaped body.

These mimics also act like wasps and bees. Many of them eat the same types of flower nectar or fruits as bees and wasps. Some of the mimics even make a buzzing sound. They also mimic the way a wasp or bee flies by hovering in the air and quickly darting here and there.

The viceroy caterpillar eats willow leaves, which are also full of toxins. Both kinds of caterpillars will still have these poisons in their bodies after they become butterflies.

Once the caterpillars have eaten and grown, they each form a chrysalis. The chrysalises of the monarch and viceroy also look very different. The monarch's chrysalis is bright green. It is large and smooth. The viceroy's chrysalis is bumpy and brown.

But when the monarch and viceroy butterflies finally come out of their chrysalises, they look almost exactly alike. Both are bright orange and black. Each has white spots lining the outside of its wings.

The only way to tell a viceroy from a monarch butterfly is a thin line. The viceroy has a black line across both of its back wings. The monarch does not. The viceroy is also a little smaller than the monarch. But these differences are not enough to help birds tell the two apart.

Looking Like the Locals

Viceroy butterflies live all over the United States. Some even live in southern Canada and in Mexico. Monarch butterflies are found in only a few of these places. Mimicry works only if the mimic looks like another animal in its area. If there are no monarchs around, it does not help the viceroy to look like one.

Wild FACT Monarch butterflies migrate, or move from one place to another. Thousands of monarchs travel between Canada and Mexico each year.

For example, viceroy butterflies in Florida look very different than in other places. The viceroy butterflies found in Florida are not bright orange and black. They are a deeper brown and black. Instead of mimicking the monarch, these viceroy butterflies mimic the queen butterfly. The queen butterfly is a close cousin of the

The queen butterfly is a close cousin of the monarch. Where there are more queen butterflies, the viceroy mimics look more like them.

monarch. There are far more queen butterflies in Florida than orange monarchs. So it makes sense that in Florida, it is better for a viceroy butterfly to look like a queen butterfly than a monarch butterfly.

25

Chapter 4

No Newt Is Good Newt

The red eft is one bad youngster! When it grows up to be an adult, it is called a red-spotted newt. And like many newts and salamanders, the red eft has toxic skin. In fact, its skin does not just taste bad—it is deadly! Its poison is enough to kill almost any animal that tries to eat it.

The red eft (left) and red salamander (right) are both toxic to other animals. Looking alike helps keep them safer.

The red eft has bright red or orange skin with several spots on its back. The bright red or orange colors warn other animals to leave the red eft alone. It is no wonder that other types of salamanders mimic the red eft's color. The red salamander is one of these.

Both the red eft and the red salamander live in the same areas. Salamanders and newts are amphibians. This means that they can live both in water and on land. They also go through a few different stages of life before becoming adults. They begin their lives in the water as eggs. After the eggs hatch, they look very similar to frog tadpoles. (Newts and salamanders do not lose their tails like tadpoles do, however.)

***Wild*FACT** Some salamanders never lose their gills. The weird-looking mudpuppy keeps its frilly gills even as an adult.

27

The baby newts and salamanders lose their gills, which help them breathe underwater. They next grow legs and lungs, which allow them to breathe on land. By now they have their bright red spotted skin.

Land Ho!

With legs and lungs, the red eft and red salamander can live on land. They can be found in large forests where lots of rain falls. Even though the red eft and red salamander live on land, they still need to be close to wet areas.

Red efts and red salamanders spend their time resting under rocks or logs, but they do not need to hide from other animals. Their bright red, poisonous skin protects them by warning predators to stay away. So predators usually leave both amphibians alone. Looking alike helps both the red eft and the red salamander stay safer. Neither the red eft or its mimic has a greater chance of being nibbled than the other.

Very Cheeky Mimic

The imitator salamander is a mimic. It is even named for its copycat style. These salamanders live in eastern Tennessee and western North Carolina. Most of them live in the Great Smoky Mountains.

There are different imitator salamanders, and they each look like another kind of salamander. Of course it all depends on what colors or markings they have. Some imitator salamanders have brown and yellow skin. They look a lot like mountain dusky salamanders.

Most imitator salamanders look like Jordan's salamanders (below). The Jordan's salamander has a black body. It also has bright red legs and cheeks. It is very poisonous to other animals. The imitator salamanders have the same black body and bright red cheeks. But that is all they have in common—imitator salamanders are not toxic to predators.

Under Its Skin

The dark spots on the back of the red eft and red salamander are the best way to tell the two animals apart. The red eft has black rings around dark red spots. The red salamander's spots are black.

Both amphibians' skin is poisonous, but the red salamander is not deadly. Its poison only stings and burns the unlucky animals that try to eat it. But the red eft is truly dangerous. Its poison can kill an animal very quickly. Like almost all salamanders and newts, the poisons are made naturally by the red eft's body. It does not get its poison from the food it eats, like some animals.

Oh, Grow Up!

The red eft does not stay very dangerous forever. It does not even stay red forever. After two or three years, the young eft turns into a full-grown red-spotted newt. Its skin changes from bright, spotted red to a dull, olive green

As an adult, the red eft is called a red-spotted newt. Not only is it not really "red" anymore, it is much less poisonous.

color. Then it moves back to water to live. Now it is also much less poisonous than it was as an eft.

This could be bad news for the red salamander. Its copycat act works only when there are red efts living nearby. After all,

Pretty and Poisonous

Some of the most poisonous animals in the world are poison dart frogs. They are most often found in rain forest jungles. There are many kinds of poison dart frogs. They all have one thing in common: They are beautifully colored. Their bright rainbow colors warn other animals of the toxins in their skin.

Even the poison dart frogs have a mimic among them. The imitator poison dart frog (left) is a tiny frog found in the jungles of Peru. It is no bigger than an adult's thumbnail. It has bright green or yellow skin, with large black dots all over its body. This color makes the imitator frog look like another dangerous poison dart frog that also lives in Peru, the Zimmerman's poison dart frog (right).

It is very hard to tell these two tiny poisonous frogs apart. Since they look like each other, neither of them has a greater chance than the other of being snapped up by a predator.

if there were no deadly red efts around, predators might learn in time that the red salamander was not as dangerous. Maybe its bad taste would be worth it for a hungry predator. But luckily for the red salamander, new red efts are always coming on land to grow into red-spotted newts. And as long as there are red efts, predators are not likely to take a chance. So, the red salamander stays safe.

Wild FACT **Most salamanders are only a few inches long, but the giant salamander can grow to more than six feet long! It is the largest amphibian anywhere in the world. It can be found in the eastern United States, China, and Japan.**

Chapter 5 The Great Pretender

It's a lion fish! It's a sole fish! It's a sea snake!
No, it is a mimic octopus. Octopuses are
known for their ability to change color. They
can look like almost any rock or coral. But the
mimic octopus takes those tricks to the next
level. It is the first octopus ever found that is
able to mimic another animal. It is also the only
animal in the world that can mimic more than
one type of animal.

Octopuses are masters of camouflage. But the mimic octopus is a great "actor," too!

Before 1998, no one had ever seen the mimic octopus. Then it was found by divers in the muddy estuaries of Indonesia. An estuary is where a river meets the ocean. The water there is part fresh and part salty. So far, this is the only place the mimic octopus has been seen.

Scientists watched this new octopus many times over two years. They took pictures and filmed movies. Everything the scientists saw surprised them.

The mimic octopus can grow up to two feet long. It is usually brown-and-white striped. Its body shape is the same as any other octopus. All octopuses are cephalopods (SEF-a-low-pods). They have a large, sac-like body, which floats behind their heads.

WILD FACT Scientists saw one female mimic octopus float on top of the water with all her legs hanging down. They think she may have been imitating a jellyfish.

An octopus uses its good eyesight and sense of touch to find prey.

There are two large eyes on top of their head. Behind those is one of the smartest brains of any ocean animal. Mimic octopuses have eight long arms like all octopuses. What they do with those arms is what makes this mimic special.

Smarty-pus

Scientists have found that the mimic octopus usually spends most of the day sitting still.

Fur and Feather Mimics

There are very few mammal or bird mimics. The main reason is that for mimicry to exist, one of the animals has to be poisonous or bad-tasting. There are no poisonous mammals or birds, right? Wrong! There are a few types of birds that are poisonous.

The hooded pitohui (PIT-oo-wee) is one of these. It lives in New Guinea. This bird has poisonous feathers and skin. It is the same type of poison found in some poison dart frogs. Scientists believe this bird gets its poison from beetles that it eats.

The hooded pitohui has a black body. It has bright red and yellow feathers around its neck and shoulders. These bright feathers tell other, harmless animals that the bird is poisonous. A few other kinds of birds in New Guinea have the same colored feathers as the hooded pitohui. This makes predators think they are poisonous, too.

It keeps its long arms tucked under itself. It sits in its sandy burrow waiting for food to pass by. Its favorite foods are small shellfish and other fish.

Sometimes the mimic octopus slowly crawls along the estuary floor. It pokes its arms into holes looking for food. When it is on the hunt, the mimic octopus looks like any other octopus. It is not trying to hide or disguise itself. But when frightened or bothered, things change. The mimic octopus changes its shape to look like dangerous ocean animals.

With its eight arms spread wide, a mimic octopus (left) can look a lot like a poisonous lionfish (right).

Sometimes the mimic octopus flattens itself out. It puts all of its arms close to its body. When swimming like this, it looks just like one of the striped sole fish found in the area. These sole fish are brown-and-white striped just like the mimic octopus. They are also often very poisonous. Large fish and sharks would most likely avoid these types of fish. So they also avoid the mimic octopus.

Other times, the mimic octopus swims with all eight arms spread wide. This makes it look like the deadly lion fish. A lion fish is also brown-and-white striped. It has large, spiny fins along its back and sides. Each spine is full of very powerful poison.

I See a Sea Snake

Scientists have seen the mimic octopus act like a sea snake several times. This is the octopus's way of keeping damselfish away. The damselfish is small but can be very aggressive. It will protect its living area, and does not want any other animals in its space. A damselfish will attack anything that comes near its home, including a mimic octopus.

One animal the damselfish is afraid of, however, is the sea snake. The damselfish can be part of a sea snake's diet. Whenever the mimic octopus is bothered by damselfish, it mimics the sea snake. The octopus puts six legs down in the sand. It lets two legs float free. This looks very much like the striped sea snakes that live in the same area.

The fact that the mimic octopus pretends to be several different animals amazes scientists. What is even more amazing is that it seems to decide what animal to mimic. Scientists watch the octopus closely. They can see that the mimic octopus changes its look to fit the situation. Scientists also realize

Wild FACT

Some fish are mimics also. The pacu is a fish found in the Amazon River in South America. It looks like its meat-eating cousin, the piranha. The pacu, however, is a gentle plant-eater.

A mimic octopus will bury its head and six of its arms, and stretch out the other two arms (left). This helps it to look like a sea snake (right).

that the mimic octopus imitates only very poisonous animals.

There is still much to learn about the mimic octopus. Scientists have to study it much longer to really know about it. One thing is for sure: It is one smart mimic!

Hiding in Plain Sight

In the animal world, mimics are masters of deception. While some animals use camouflage to hide, mimics take their tricks even further.

Their defense is to look scarier, yuckier, or bigger than they really are. Mimics might look like something dangerous. They might look like something disgusting. They may even be dangerous or disgusting themselves! However they look, their copycat ways keep them safe and able to hide in plain sight.

Mimicry works because most predators will not take a chance to find out if the mimicking animal is dangerous or not. When it works, mimicry is an amazing animal defense.

"Keep your friends close. Keep your enemies closer." This is a famous saying from General Sun Tzu in 400 BC. It is a belief that has been used by militaries for years. We know it as "spying." Many times, the best way to find out more about people is to mimic them. Spies risk their lives as human mimics.

In almost every war, spies have played a big role in helping to learn about an enemy. Spies have to know how to dress, talk, and act like the enemy. They have to learn the language of the country in which they are spying. They also have to study the ways of the people they are spying on. Many times, spies will wear disguises to look like the local people. Costumes and makeup help change their appearance. The only way to be safe is by being a perfect mimic.

Like spies, undercover police officers do their best to blend in. This helps them catch criminals in the act!

43

Any mistake could mean disaster, just like in the animal world.

Throughout history, most countries have used spies at one time or another. Many times, the spies are people who live in the enemy country. This works well because they already know the language and customs. These spies are hard to notice. Sometimes a country will find enemy spies to work for them. These are called double-agents.

No matter who the spy is, their job is to find out information. They go undercover to learn government and military plans and secrets. This helps the country they are working for know what the enemy is up to. Today, human spies are still used, but less often. Satellites and computers do more of the spy work now. They have taken over much of the dangerous work that was once done by human spies.

The Predator looks a lot like a regular plane, but it is an aircraft used by the military for spying. It gathers information and sends it to computers on the ground.

amphibian—A cold-blooded animal that can live both on land and in water, such as a frog or salamander.

camouflage—When an animal uses its appearance or color to blend in with its surroundings.

cephalopod—A type of animal, such as an octopus or squid, that has several long arms and a very large head.

chrysalis—A hard case in which a caterpillar turns into a butterfly.

defense—Protection against an attack.

eye spots—Dark, round markings on an animal's body that look like eyes.

mimic—An animal that has the appearance of a more dangerous animal in order to fool predators.

mimicry—Having the appearance of a more dangerous animal in order to fool predators.

predator—An animal that hunts and eats other animals.

prey—An animal that is a food source for other animals.

self-mimicry—A defense in which part of an animal's body looks like another part, such as a false head.

toxic—Poisonous.

venom—A substance produced by certain animals such as snakes. It becomes toxic when injected into a victim, usually through biting.

Further Reading

Books

Hoff, Mary King. *Mimicry and Camouflage*. Mankato, Minn.: Creative Education, 2002.

Jenkins, Steve. *Living Color*. Boston: Houghton Mifflin, 2007.

Kalman, Bobbie. *What Are Camouflage & Mimicry?* New York: Crabtree Publishing, 2001.

Purser, Bruce. *Jungle Bugs: Masters of Camouflage and Mimicry*. Richmond Hill, Ont.: Firefly Books, 2003.

Internet Addresses

Animals on Defense: Copycats
http://oncampus.richmond.edu/academics/education/projects/webunits/adaptations/mimicry.html

Kidzone: The Monarch Butterfly
http://www.kidzone.ws/animals/monarch_butterfly.htm

Index